DIVING INTO LEADERSHIP

Motivating Others

DIVING INTO LEADERSHIP

Motivating Others

Tim Vancamp

Diving Into Leadership: Motivating Others

Copyright © 2018 Tim Vancamp

Cover designed by Christabel Ogbomon

Disclaimer

First Printing: 2018

ISBN: 9781717749185

Dedication

In beloved memory of two heroes,

Gerda Beeris, my mother,

Clara Espin, my mother-in-law

They infused me with the love for life and a

sense of never-ending spirit, courage and fearlessness.

*"As I headed out for a night dive, I saw the sunset-colored waves
extinguish on the beach, but with subdued memories I can see your
sun rays surfing the sea towards me. Far away but always near me."*

~ Tim Vancamp ~

&

Two champions,

Robert Vancamp, my father

Anton Hernandez, my father-in-law

They are a great inspirational statue in my life, whose
perpetual encouragement and support has been a source
of strength, motivation and enthusiasm

Contents

INTRODUCTION

"I dive because I'd rather look back at life, saying "I can't believe I did that" instead of "if only I had.""

~ Unknown ~

Diving - scuba diving - is a sport that most people do for pure enjoyment and first-class experience of the underwater world; a world so different from ours and undoubtedly astonishing. Diving is a means of undergoing a new environmental experience that will change your thoughts of 'the normal'. I can categorically say that humans take seeing, hearing and even breathing for granted. All these can no longer be taken for granted when one indulges in an environment filled with water. Diving changes the notion about a lot, and teaches a lot!

People around the world have taken interest in this fun and exciting sport because it offers immense benefits in addition to the memorable experience one gets from getting to know the sea and the various creatures of the water. Going forward, diving is also a great way to stay healthy. Let's have a look at some of the reasons why diving is a good choice for almost anyone.

Benefits of Diving

- **Overall Physical Fitness**

Because diving takes place in the water, unlike other sports, the diver gets a complete body workout. This is because there is natural resistance in the water and although movement may seem free, calories are burnt as a result of internal resistance.

- **Stress Reducer**

Diving gives whichever individual the opportunity to get away from hectic and most probably stressful schedules that come loaded into their everyday lives. The sound of water itself is known to be advantageous to the human health. In addition to this, the time spent being weightless in the water is one big stress-reliever itself.

- **Improves Awareness & Concentration**

This sport plays an important role in increasing attention rate, awareness as well as concentration. Here's the thing: in order to swim underwater, one needs to be very focused, attentive and careful. This, in turn, helps to increase control over body movements and the big picture here is that one begins to pay attention to details in the outside world.

• **Flexibility, Strength & More**

Perhaps one of the prominent benefits offered by diving, it facilitates flexibility and true strength while also enhancing quickness of the feet. More so, individuals who dive on a regular basis are likely not to have strokes or heart attacks as it helps with reducing blood pressure.

• **Enhances Socialization**

Diving has a way of stimulating trust, communication, as well as responsibility (especially when in groups or with someone). Partners share a common bond over their joint experience and interest which breeds effective socialization. This leads us to the next benefit which will be our focus in the next few pages.

• **Hones Leadership Skills**

Right from communication to taking responsibilities and more, diving is more or less like a course taken to build one's leadership skills. Why? You are taught how to be a true leader, amidst the woes of the new world and unseen circumstances. Leaders need oxygen, right? They've got to keep breathing; in the toughest of situations, breathe and move on. The underwater teaches you not to ever forget to breathe. In the rescue diver course, you'll learn to: stop, think, breathe, then act so panic is unlikely and appropriate measures are implemented or taken.

Furthermore, while diving, talking becomes a challenge so divers are taught to communicate through hand signals. A team – regardless the kind – needs a system of communicating in a simple manner as it helps leaders to understand the situation at hand without having to hold a meeting or go through several paperwork. Simply by paying attention to teammates' signals, leaders are able to learn a lot about their system.

Now, what happens when you can't find your partner in the deep? Divers are taught not to panic, as this could bring regrettable consequences. In relation to leadership, forget how many feet of deep shit the challenge looks like; leaders are expected to stay calm and take cognizant decisions. Lastly on this note, diving teaches unarguably courage in all shades.

In general, learning to dive is like learning to fly. One has to understand the necessities and start to learn from the very first step and take it forward from there slowly. There are lots of diving institutions around ready to assist with their lessons and equipment. The secret, however, is finding which one is the right one for you. As well as who your right fit as an instructor, thus your leader and coach, is.

Learning to dive largely depends on one's ability and need, as well as the purpose behind the decision. Whether you want to be a professional diver or simply want to try it out for recreational purposes, decide first! Actually, you need to go through the recreational training stages first (open water diver, advanced open water diver and rescue diver), before you can step into the professional training curriculum.

Essentially, anyone as of the age of 10 is capable of taking dive initiations or courses. Actually, as of 8 years old you can already take a dive initiation which is commonly called "bubble maker" and as of the age of 10 one can start junior courses similar to the adult courses but specified to youth with applicable rules like for example maximum dive depths and obligatory guidance rules. My daughter for example, is 12 years old, at the time of writing, and just finished her junior open water diver and advanced open water certification in less than a year time. She, already holds several specialization certificates like: altitude diving, buoyancy, emergency oxygen provider, underwater navigation and night diving specialty. Fully determined to move up the ladder to higher diving levels, she already shows some traits of leadership, which will be further explained in this book. The starter pack for any diving lesson is the desire to learn, interest, good health, great body condition and self-determination. The typical diving lesson will begin its course with theories mixed with practical sessions until you are fully grounded to go with a guide or with friends to explore the magical underwater world while in the meantime perfecting team building skills as well. Ultimately, new divers are awarded a certification meaning they can go ahead and begin their diving career after the necessary training path is successfully finished or enjoy the recreational activity anywhere in the world.

Sooner or later that leadership position you have dreamt of will become vacant at your workplace and you have worked very hard and know you want to take that role, but... Ask yourself some questions: Do people like working with me? Do I have their trust? Would they follow me if I were to be the leader, or in that position? Am I business and non-business savvy enough in the right areas? Do I possess the right hard and soft skills to be in that role? How am I perceived by others? Did I develop people to step into my position? Do I take big decisions, risks, make mistakes because I learn from everything I am involved in? Do I fit in? Do I have a good track record? ...

Am I a LEADER?

In this first volume you will find answers to help you transform yourself and conduct yourself like a leader. Position yourself for each new promotion and transform yourself from an average employee or person to an indispensable (corporate) leader with the help of this book. Angles taken both from the corporate world as well as the diving world will help you further fine-tune, improve and create those skill sets and behaviors necessary to reach the leadership positions you aspire.

Now, let's go ahead and delve completely into how diving can be a major sauce for effective leadership. Start today with home schooling yourself to be an effective leader, as you already have the basis and can go all the way. Undergo the adventure of the leadership journey. Where you are today is the result of your decisions and actions in the past, now it's time to build your future. Your future starts with the decisions and actions you take, what you accomplish and the changes you make, today. So, why wait any longer? Dive into leadership, now!

Tim Vancamp

Tim Vancamp

Acknowledgements

This work would not have been possible without the professional help of Ms. Cassie Bridget. Her passion, dedication and perseverance have led to the accomplishment of this book to finally publish it.

I'm grateful for a number of friends and colleagues, who have been both an inspiration as well as an example which led to the idea and topics of this first volume.

Nobody has been more important to put me in the pursuit of this book than the members of my family. I would like to thank my parents; whose love and guidance are with me in whatever I pursue. My ultimate role models.

Experiences are truly appreciated only if obstacles are overcome, problems solved, and you learn to compromise, first of all with brothers. I could never have written this book without the inspiring help and life lessons from my brothers Guy and Steven.

And above all, my life wouldn't have been as full and rich as it is without the infinite love and support of my wife, Carolina, and two wonderful children, Amber and Max, who provide infinite inspiration.

Tim Vancamp

CHAPTER 1:

HIGH ENERGY

Tim Vancamp

High Energy

"When you are enthusiastic about what you do,
you feel this positive energy. It's very simple."

~ Paulo Coelho ~

There is a big difference between merely growing into the position of a leader and actually being a meaningful, quality and effective leader. Yes, holding a position has always meant that you were either willing to be selected or able, then elected or ascended to some specific position but, hey! Being a true leader is actually based on a rare combination of abilities, assets and skills in order to make a difference in your team as well as for the entire organization. Being in a leadership position doesn't give you the right to be lazy, on the contrary. A leadership position gives you the possibilities, the authorization to do more. This implies ultimately that a leader should channel his/her energy to create possibilities and solutions and serve those in need of guidance and this positive energy, no matter whether it is a person, a team, a business unit or an entire organization, a group of divers any other group of people.

Diving has never been for the faint at heart! Divers are charged with high energy to face the unseen and the unknown. These individuals have seen a need to understand the necessities required to go deep into the water and proceed further, with the highest level of **ENERGY** and **COURAGE.** That's who a leader should be. Fearless and daring, with every strength he can muster, though with a solid and sound cognition.

Do You Possess the Energy to Be a Quality Leader?

Answer these...

1. **On Empathy:** So, I ask, what purpose is served if you merely thrust ahead, without putting into consideration the needs, perceptions, and objectives of your constituents? Will you be ready, willing and able to give listening ears to discover what is needed – and wanted – by your teammates to proceed with consistency and the right degree of empathy?

2. **On Necessities:** Will you be able to prioritize and positively address team members, in a way that motivates them to focus and care more about the joint goal to be achieved? Will you motivate them

to be more involved in the task at hand and forthwith prepare them for a level of future leadership? In order to motivate them as you must, this must be done in an energetic, focused way.

3. **On Endurance:** There is so much divers endure when they are 100 feet into the water; many become frustrated, but what makes a true leader in situations like this? Pseudo-divers won't proceed at this point, as they lack commitment and a high level of endurance, which true leaders need. A real leader searches for excellence, never settling for the 'good-enough' or the average performance. Are you willing to endure challenging situations, even if there seems to be no headway?

4. **On Reliability:** Will your teammates be able to rely on you at down-times? Are you able to quickly come to their aid just when needed? While leaders must provide relevant direction, they are only able to achieve the desired impact if they do so consistently with great energy. Will your constituents find you reliable and worth following?

5. **On Goodwill:** Doing what is best for the team as well as goodwill can be a tough combination. However, groups must undergo relevant and consistent growth or risk unsustainability in the

long run. Are you willing to do an effective combination of goodwill and team needs?

6. **About You:** Rid yourself of playing the blame game so that you can attract team members to work together in unity. Those who blame and complain end up failing to behave as real leaders whilst totally blind towards seeking viable solutions. As a leader, it is always up to you, and you must take personal responsibility!

Why Does This Even Matter?

How a leader expresses and articulates his vital vision while taking time and making necessary efforts to continue to push forward with utmost degree of genuine empathy, is often what makes the major difference. Pardon the Latin-laid pieces of tongue-twisting literature, all I'm saying is, when leaders are energetic and this can be recognized by stakeholders as well as teammates, they become quick to enhance and improve their abilities for the best result possible. It all lies in the thirst to genuinely push forward; of course, with high energy!

ENERGY is an important element of any leader; this is probably what you would be taught first in a diving school – how to garner energy for effective diving – and so does it apply to leadership. With that in mind, let's look briefly into why the quality and consistency of a leader's energy matter much, in relation to where we are coming from.

1. **Enlightenment:** Being a source of motivation to others is an essential component of quality leadership. It is required of true leaders to focus on what is needed and push forward, consistently, in order to enlighten their teammates as well as to communicate effectively their goals and priorities. Furthermore, in the quest to enlighten stakeholders, leaders explain why these goals are important to their organization. Pushing harder with so much energy, leaders attain their highest level of excellence on each micro-goal; rather than settling for the average or the good-enough. This is what differentiates true leaders (who serve effectively) from the rest of the pack. In short, we say this is energy channeled into enlightenment.

2. **Needs:** The only yardstick for measuring how far one has gone is by recognizing feats as well as drawbacks; and as such, one is able to understand what is needed to achieve the next goal at hand. How can anyone make any significant difference if he does not focus on goals, priorities and needs? In your team, whose agenda will you emphasize on;

your very personal agenda, or that which would benefit those that you lead?

3. **Empathy:** If you are not an inspiration to others, how then will they see a need to stay committed? This can only be done when one prioritizes, listens effectively and then learns the goals and perceptions of those he serves. This way, they feel the leader really cares about them and as this high level of energy is felt by everyone, the leader gains a plus reputation at enriching their experience.

4. **Reinvigorate:** Energetic leaders reinvigorate those who might have gotten *burnt-out* during the course of certain tasks so as to reach out to them and gather the group towards being better and more meaningful. As a matter of fact, one will only make a significant difference for the better when he seeks the best and most relevant solution – which in most cases requires input from every member of the team. The need to refresh, reach out and reinvigorate cannot be overstretched!

5. **Growth & Goodwill:** Of course, the default notion is that leaders carry the burden to seek growth for the good of the group. Yes, right! However, it is even more important that leaders proceed consistently in a way that is accented with

goodwill. This should not be done because of said promises but because of the planning and strategy on ground. In diving, it is a good rule of thumb to always check up on your partner; and suggest good movement trails as you move along.

6. **Back to YOU:** As long as you are a leader, it is always up to you. Sounds like a cliché right? There is no better truth behind leadership. You send the cue, others follow. Deep within the water, divers take extra caution and watch out for their buddies; if you find a better view to dive into, be the lead. If you see something that seems obscure, call the attention of others. That's what leaders do! Certainly, they will be thankful for it and trust you further. When one is genuinely energetic, his personal strengths, vision and energy make other people better! Clear communication and seamless transmission of this energy set a leader in the position to say yes to the best possible results each time.

"Leadership is not just about giving energy ... it's unleashing other people's energy."

~ Paul Polman ~

All of these sums up to say, "If you hope to be an effective leader, you are responsible to push forward, with the highest level of **ENERGY**, which could be the point of inspiration to others in a significant way". So, are you up to this task?

How Leaders Can Increase Their Personal Energy

So, you have identified the need to be a leader full of energy as with diving where coordination, trust flow and of course, physical strength is needed. What next now? Taking charge and sustaining the energy!

Leaders' energy is divided into two dimensions - internal and external. **The internal dimension** is what occurs as a result of internal values, beliefs and attitude. In this case, we have elements like curiosity, opportunities, sense of self, optimism, etc. Most highly successful and energetic people usually don't appear to be energetic on the external. However, what they possess on the inside (the internal energy) is at its peak; this is the energy that keeps them going from within.

The external dimension is that which is seen and perceived by others through a leader's behavior.

Well, many people may agree that part of high energy, both internal and external may have come from genes – saying some people's motors are programmed to run faster. That could be true, but let's face it, the biggest elements of creating energy are passion, focus, commitment and accomplishment.

Did you know even that exercise is a fuel for recharging the internal batteries? From a small survey, many leaders have shown interest in exercises as a way of describing how the two dimensions cooperate with each other or sometimes, against. Some leaders have a way of forcing themselves to meet their commitment as it lifts them up in many cases. Introspectively, these leaders are proud that they fought through series of negative vibes eventually, in order to do what they had the commitment to do. While their performance level may have suffered severely, the fact that they were able to keep to their commitment energizes them on both dimensions. You know, just like the conventional exercises, it feels so good when you are finished!

The Energy Creation/Sustainability Nuggets

One notable characteristic of divers is how they are able to keep pressing on without giving in to the fear of the unknown. Naturally, they are going into a new world they have never been to or are not used to. They should reconsider diving deeper, right? No. They don't. Leaders increase their personal energy by pushing forward; by pressing on, even when obstacles and negative emotions seem to be all over them. They don't stop! Pressing onward is what drives them. Action creates energy.

"Nothing succeeds like success". The truth in this cannot be matched! Leaders learn overtime to create and renew energy through accomplishments. This spans from personal accomplishments down to organizational, group and family levels. This doesn't imply leaders just look for easy goals, or easy to solve problems. On the contrary, if you want to feel accomplished, then goals, targets and even problems need to change, be different, be raised and at times even stretched. It is also a kind of training and adaptation process to the environment, just like divers adapt to changing conditions and environments. Just like in diving, the more you practice, the more it of a natural habit it becomes. Master skills, knowledge, attitudes, emotions and everything you will find in this book to become a better leader and pull energy that comes from these accomplishments. Be an awesome problem solver and it will channel your energy into reaching positive outcomes that will further raise your energy level. In fact, for leaders it becomes kind of a hobby to look for accomplishments as a means of sustaining and scaling their energy, as well as that of other people in the team. Perhaps this explains why divers are quick to celebrate their success in groups once they are out of the water; even if it was just a 5-minute diving session. This is also derived from the fact that divers are very well prepared before the dive by planning, briefing, checking and double-checking as well as sticking to the plan which channels that positive energy into an accomplishment or reached goal after each successful dive.

PRO TIP

Divers plan their dive and dive their plan! Effective planning and meticulous execution actively creates energy.

Leaders have a flair for being inspired by others. Simply, they take inspiration from the pleasure and achievements (no matter how little) of others. This is because they have it at the back of their minds that *there is plenty for everybody* and *together everyone achieves more.*

Leaders believe that breaking out − committing to something they have never done before, can be petrifying, yet, energizing. It doesn't have to be climbing the tallest mountain, it could be going deep down, saying hello to sharks face-to-face. The keyword and most important to them is that it is "new". New places, new sports, new mental challenges, etc. Leaders don't see "new" as threatening or an obstacle, but rather look at it as a welcomed challenge and an opportunity to embrace, ultimately to achieve that accomplishment.

Similar to the piece above, leaders are travelers. Going to a place they have not been to before is their forte. A place they are not in the position of a leader, where the food is different, language and sometimes means of communication as with divers underwater. Embracing all of this is a great way to feel alive and energetic!

Leaders take it upon themselves to give and give back. They are energized by the experience of giving their talent, energy and their passion to others. They are sacrificial givers − giving without any expectations of a return.

Technically, they are richer for doing this; because they get rewarded with renewed energy.

Leaders secure the time of their people. They are aware of possible distractions that can take the energy out of team member's endeavors so they make it a priority to keep their people protected from value- and energy-eating habits that could come up.

Leaders work with every member of their team to create goals that fit perfectly into the common goal or vision. This entails that you facilitate people with the tools, processes, information and knowledge to set the goals in a way that they may be perceived as rather simple, though actually more challenging and complex when looked upon primarily. A leader uses his/her translational skills to simplify complexity. They ensure the common goal is a simple one to work with and have every member align their personal goals with it. More so, leaders fight to keep the journey of achieving these goals as simple as possible. The idea is to reach goals that create energy and not have a process destroying it all.

PRO TIP

Leaders communicate and keep communicating. Just when they think they have communicated enough, they feel as though they need to communicate more. Effective communication actively creates energy.

Leaders share every piece of information and knowledge they have. They don't hoard! This is the biggest part of carrying teammates along and it goes a long way for having (quick) success. They want their people to know the status quo because they know they can get relevant and effective help from team members if they know the exact situation of things at any particular moment. And from this status quo they learn to challenge it for the better.

Finally, leaders promote optimism in themselves and every other person. They begin their day with the belief that something special – something good – will come their way. They know negative expectations in themselves and others brings low energy so they stay positive.

Positive energy creation can be as simple as saying good morning with a genuine smile, every day you get to work or when you encounter someone at the elevator for example, no matter who they are. "Good morning", "hello", "hi", ...

Yes, it is that simple, and yet not everyone does it and especially leaders should, otherwise I wouldn't consider that a leader. Leading by example is appropriate in this case. It's easy, it's free and it hardly costs you anything, not even energy, as you can do it while walking towards your office for example. Better yet start when you wake up and say "good morning" to your spouse. I bet not everyone does it. If you have troublesome thoughts, don't feel optimal or whatever it may be that preoccupies you, that is not an excuse not to be polite and smile. Others may not be aware what is going on, they may not have a bad day or they simply don't care because they themselves have their own things going on in their (private) life. As a leader you control that negative energy and you can and have to transform it into a positive one. No matter how tough it may be, always say good morning with a smile for this matter or else, just work from home that day. Simple as that! Saying "good morning" without a smile and a drooped face is a contradiction between the verbal and non-verbal communication of the message and will be interpreted differently and/or wrongly. So, don't do it.

Your personal energy is critical to your success as well as that of the organization/group you are leading. Without a high level of both internal and external energy, success becomes difficult to find. Although, on the surface, it might appear that action takes energy away; however, the reverse is the case in reality.

Diving into Leadership: Motivating Others

Tim Vancamp

CHAPTER 2:

INTUITIVENESS

Tim Vancamp

Intuitiveness

---

*"The best leaders are readers of people. They have
the intuitive ability to understand others by
discerning how they feel and recognizing what
they sense."*

~ John C. Maxwell ~

W hen we think of someone we consider to be intuitive, we envisage someone who has a rare combination of judgment, wisdom, effectiveness and understanding. Intuition is a 'connect' to the universal and intelligent life force that exists within an individual. It is deep wisdom. It is an inner knowing. It is an internal library of knowledge and understanding.

Wouldn't it be nice if all leaders proved themselves worthy of all of these qualities before they are awarded any position? Or how then shall we belittle a man courageous enough to go deep into an unknown world where danger lurks amidst uncertainty – yes, I'm talking about diving here. Without great intuition, divers are more exposed to danger and should never try the sport for anything. So great, if you are already considering diving, this means you are preparing to take self-intuition-lessons for every time you go into the water. Once again, here's a big chance that diving prepares you to be a successful leader!

With that said, if every leader were capable of seeing, hearing and identifying the bigger picture as well as foreseeing obstacles then going further to seek solutions (rather than playing the blame game), wouldn't most organizational settings be better and more relevant? Now, if you want to be a leader, ask yourself if you've got the power of INTUITIVENESS.

The INTUITION Cookbook

1. **Introspection; insight:** Checking up ourselves from the neck-up, and being objectively introspective is certain to highlight for us our strengths and weaknesses – at least so we could use our strong points to the best of our abilities. The same would provide one of the most useful tools of leadership, which is relevant insight (and understanding of it). Conceiving, perceiving and understanding fully what must be addressed is most beneficial to the leader and the entire group.

2. **Timeliness:** Are you the *LASTMAN* kind of person? Do you address present and upcoming ´ in

a timely manner? Or do you just focus on already-addressed issues which are no longer relevant? Intuition and timeliness go hand-in-hand. What is the use of the inner wisdom when it doesn't come to play at the right time?

3. **Needs:** Are you able to focus on NEEDS and concerns with the necessary priority they require? Don't get caught up in petty distractions. Great leaders are needs-oriented people! In addition to focusing on just what is right for the team, 'great leaders' are humans like other people; so, they rid themselves of dictatorship role to the barest minimum. They teach. They coach. They inspire. They are smart enough to listen to their followers on how everyone can best solve the challenge at hand. As Steve Jobs once said:

"It doesn't make sense to hire smart people and then tell them what to do: we hire smart people, so they can tell us what to do".

~ Steve Jobs ~

---

4. **Intents; imagination:** Be sure you are focused on serving people even as you examine your personal motivations. Leaders are followers with authority;

they lead to serve. Don't be stuck with the same-old worn tactics, take on new approaches as you discover new challenges as well. Great imaginations could mean great intuition and consequently, great leadership!

5. **Useful; usable:** Successful leaders understand that not everything should be given equal relevance or importance. A great leader must be able to differentiate between what is useful and usable from what is not.

6. **Time-tested approach:** While it is necessary to consider alternatives with an open mind, leaders should not abandon time-tested approaches that have been tested to work and will continue to show relevance in their field. An individual who is able to balance this, while taking advantage of present trends as well as great imagination is worthy of being called a leader; a successful one at that.

7. **Nuances:** Intuition becomes more relevant and needed when it comes to understanding that different organizations, groups, teams, individuals, etc. have their own unique characteristics and therefore, leaders must accept and use necessary nuances relevant enough to address the specific setting they lead.

8. **Integrity:** As a leader, it is a good rule of thumb to never abandon absolute integrity for a mere short-term or quick fix to challenges. Without your integrity, are there other reasons anyone would follow you?

Similar to effective communication in diving, one does not simply do what will aggravate the situation sooner or at a later time. Leaders calm down to apply the best fix that will bring them out of a situation, never to return again.

PRO TIP

Be consistent by conscious choice in your words, behaviors and actions. Be honest in those three as well and strive for your "wholeness" (integer in Latin means whole and complete). People will notice you are in integrity.

You see, intuition is a practical tool that comes in handy when we have to deal with life's experiences. It brings helpful decisions, solutions to problems and yes, inspires ideas. The intuitive self is an amazing resource and gift that we can use to enrich the quality of our lives, work, activities, etc.

Wear Your Gloves, Let's Get Dirty...

Some people think of intuition as a special gift, which certain special people have, and many others do not. Wrong! We all have the ability of intuitiveness. Perhaps these thinkers have only had experiences where they felt they were not able to contribute to intuition. How about you see if any of these (below) has happened to you before now?

- Having an instinct for something. You knew the best decision to take at certain times and it paid off!

- The phone rang; you knew it was Jessica.

- You are out for lunch, you feel someone is boring their eyes into you and when your turn to confirm, he/she looks away.

- The "gut feeling" that something is about to happen.

The aforementioned are simple examples of how intuition occurs naturally in our everyday lives.

Admittedly though, some people are more intuitive than others. This is because these people see it necessary to ponder more on things so of course, their reward is better intuition. Inventors and leaders are likely examples. They ask questions like "How can I get this to work?", "How can I develop this idea?" "What is the best fix for this situation?" "Why did it happen?"

As soon as they ponder and begin to relax on these, solutions tend to flow out of their daydreams. That is exactly when you see the sudden elation on their faces because a viable solution has come to mind. Or they drill down the problem to find the root cause and start working on solutions to mediate the problem while trying to fix it in a way they prevent it from happening again in the future. They focus on the permanent solution rather than finding a quick fix or temporary solution. People who appreciate intuitiveness are dynamic and enthusiastic about living. They are exciting people too.

Intuition also comes in form of connection with other people. Say you had that "gut feeling" you needed to call someone on phone for no particular reason. You begin worrying about that person but have no idea why. These connections can get really strong, depending on your level of intuitive ability. Here's a quick example of how powerful the people-connection can be:

Cheryl's mother was particularly intuitive with people. She had a passion for knowing what's going on with her immediate family.

One night, she couldn't find peace within herself and walked the hallway throughout the night. She had the "gut feeling" that something was wrong with Cheryl's step-brother in New Zealand. Well, both she and her daughter stayed in Australia all through the while – so this explains that distance is no barrier to "checking up" on others.

In the morning, she picked up her phone to call him, only to find out that he has been away for the weekend. She then left him a message to give her a call back at once! Saturday that week, Cheryl's step-brother called back and explained to their mom how he's camped near a riverside with his wife. On Friday night, a storm had swept in and they got caught up on the patch of the land surrounded by an additional channel of water created by the same storm. The only route for survival was to swim to shore. They had lost all their belongings at this point and their car was about four hours away. They were rescued by a team of lifesavers eventually.

The story ended on a good note but as you can see, Cheryl's mother couldn't settle unless she knew that they were fine. INTUITION!

It is quite unfortunate that many people do not know how to use their intuition. They sometimes see it as something for the "gifted" but in truth, it is a gift for everyone.

Something to ponder:

Wouldn't you find value in being able to suggest the best solutions to your problems? Being gifted with inspired ideas, thoughts and having the pass to your greatest potential. We all have this amazing power; all we need to do is create self-awareness within and set our mind to harness it.

Intuitive guidance can be anything from a small feeling to a strong message. The good news about the inner-self is that it is consistent and will keep making efforts to get your attention until you finally give in.

Intuition in most forms, comes from being connected with others (people or things). Mediums, psychics and spiritual healers get their intuitive messages from:

Clairaudience: process of hearing inspired thoughts

Clairvoyance: process of seeing a clear imagination or picture

Clairessence: process of sensing smells which are necessarily not present

Empathy: feeling the energy of other people

Dreaming: You know, the feeling that you have seen 'something' before.

The gift of intuitiveness is too precious to be limited by any belief whatsoever – that certain people possess it. Stop it already! Intuition is available to everyone. Commit to an everyday awareness of how your inner-self transmits information to you, so that even you, can have greater access to your faculty of intuitiveness.

5 facts that block us from following our intuition:

1. The fear of knowing what we know already.

2. We feel that we know what is best for us already.

3. Many-a-times, intuition does not appeal to the logical sense or we simply cannot explain it to other people.

4. We become afraid of other people's judgment or what they will think about if we follow our intuition.

5. From childhood, we were not really supported to trust our inner-self.

Ways to Develop Your Intuition

Try out meditation techniques

Take time out every day to experience and appreciate silence. Find a comfortable meditation technique and calm your body with it. Feel free to release your need to think and investigate everything; knowing that the best information comes right from deep within.

Provoke your inner-self with questions

By asking yourself questions, your intuition will reply with necessary answers. Try as much not to think or analyze the question to ask, just ask and hand it over to the intuition lab. Do remember also that intuitive messages will only come out of the blue when you are in a relaxed state, meditating or daydreaming. Busy people tend to receive intuitive messages less. Sometimes, these messages just drop just when we are about to sleep. It is a good rule of thumb to have a pen and a paper by the bedside for events like this. Don't hope that you will remember intuitive messages by the morning. It hardly comes back again.

Or why not, go diving! No distractions from emails, phone calls, people jumping into your office etc.

"If you need a moment to think. Go diving and you will have a few minutes of peace and quiet."

~ Ronnie Lampole ~

PRO TIP

Probe yourself with any question you wish to have an answer to. For example, "What exactly is my life goal?", "How can I achieve this goal?", "What should I do right now to resolve this issue?" "How can I improve that process?"

RELAX and have a moment of PEACE!

As a matter of fact, every answer is within you. So, learn to trust your internal guidance as it is capable of leading you to the direction of your highest potential.

Stay open to new opportunities

In order to accept what the inner-self has to show you, you have to be open to the gift initially. Sometimes you may try so hard to "receive" but end up with nothing but your own consciously made-up messages; it's fine. This happens when we concentrate rather than let go but you just have to pretend like you care not! Just relax and stay open. It is in this moment of peace that intuitive messages come at best.

One valuable lesson to learn about being intuitive is that it is never forced. We need to allow it to come out in its own accord. Therefore, by all means, have the readiness to tune into it then let go. Once again, note that intuition steps in just when you least expect.

Intuition is like having a mentor who has searched you and knows you intimately. It will always be available to you. It waits patiently for you to let go and tap into the wealth of your inner resources. It gives you amazing guidance and wonderful solutions to problems. All you have to do is ask!

Nurture this relationship with your inner self and give yourself time to develop these skills. It helps greatly to beat the unknown or fear of uncertainty.

Tim Vancamp

CHAPTER 3:

MATURITY

Tim Vancamp

Maturity

"Maturity is the ability to think, speak and act your feelings within the bounds of dignity. The measure of your maturity is how spiritual you become during the midst of your frustrations."

~ Samuel Ullman ~

When you hear the word "maturity", what comes to mind? Does it sound like 'old' and 'boring'? Someone who has no fun in their lives? Do you imagine that maturity is something to be avoided at all costs, simply because it demands responsibility?

Well, no. Maturity is a lot more.

Okay, that's fine. Now, let's break the common misconception about maturity in general and see what it actually is.

The dictionary has tons of definitions for maturity. I particularly like the one that says it is "fully developed powers of mind and body". This thing called maturity can sometimes be fleeting and tough to sustain but when we have it, it can be a magical experience. Here are some ideas of what maturity might actually mean:

- **Maturity might mean having shareable wisdom.** I am not saying that one has to become a busybody sticking his nose into other people's businesses. It does not mean giving unwanted advice. It also does not mean having a way of manipulating one's way into giving opinions. Wisdom, in this case, is about sharing life experience in such a way that (people who desire the information) can make satisfying and life-affirming choices for their own lives. Maybe you have learned how to communicate effectively in relationships or how to end up being happy at what you do, pass on the knowledge to people the most natural way possible. Think of maturity as having wisdom to share.

- **Maturity is not reactive.** Maturity gives an edge to see things from a higher perspective. In this regard, you take responsibility for your reactions and give up playing the blame game. Stop looking for excuses to be angry at people, things and the past. Rather than seeing others as "mean", mature people understand the pain they are driven by.

- **Maturity is accepting 100% responsibility.** Speak of the devil... Of course, maturity needs you to own every one of your actions, interactions, results, happiness and what not? Maturity needs you to be responsible for your life.

- **Maturity identifies beyond the self.** The world does not revolve around you, one person. You are not the center of the universe. The mature person allows others to express their own feelings, gives up manipulation and seeks a willing cooperation from others.

Maturity means a lot of positive and exciting things. It is about a lot of things altogether and if you have it, you are on a set path to mental and emotional freedom.

Leaders are not likely to succeed if they do not project credibility and maturity at handling things. In fact, emotional maturity is one of the key prerequisites of being a leader. People are not just going to be inspired by someone who they do not find trustworthy, authoritative, reliable and of course, mature enough to handle situations.

Maturity – Who Will You Lead Without It?

One really unfortunate way of killing credibility is through emotional outbursts. A leader who cannot control himself/herself cannot motivate other people. Everything begins with emotional maturity!

The first point I need to pass is that emotional maturity is not intended for gauging others. It is only for gauging ourselves and improving how we respond to stress and emotional situations.

As leaders attempt to motivate others, they run into frustrating situations. Frustration, just in case you don't know, is anger caused by being inhibited from attaining one's goals. You want to agree with me that we don't always meet our set goals in due time, each time. Unless you've got superpowers. How a leader responds to situations like this is where emotional maturity comes to play.

Back in the deep of the water, when a diver's buddy experiences some sort of mishap, the last thing on his mind should be panicking. He needs to handle the situation with utmost maturity otherwise, he could end up being as unfortunate as the original victim. If he allows his emotions to step in before his maturity, he risks a lot of bad things.

Emotional maturity exists in 3 levels:

If I allow my emotions to take over and control how I respond to situations, I am said to have a **low emotional maturity**.

If I am now aware of my emotions and able to keep them at arm's length from controlling me when responding to situations, then I am said to have demonstrated an **intermediate maturity.**

If I am able to demonstrate my emotions without giving them the power to control me, then I exhibit a **high emotional maturity**.

Seems shady, yes? Here's an illustration:

Assume that I have an eight-year-old son who occasionally frustrates me – or shall I put it this way, that I occasionally allow myself to be frustrated by him? If I blindly lose my temper and start yelling at him immediately, then I am certainly being controlled by my emotions and I have low emotional maturity. At this point, I am out of control and will not have any effective ways of dealing with him. More, I could be exhibiting an intermediate emotional maturity if I calmly tell him to go to his room and wait for us both to calm down then iron-out the issue at that comfortable time. Finally, I will be quite more effective if I express in my tone how angry I am but still remain in control. That's high level of emotional maturity right there.

A leader who has mastered his emotional maturity is not only able to control his/her emotions but is also aware of the emotions of his team members and respond accordingly.

PRO TIP

Always remember that when attempting to motivate other people, your feelings mean less to them than their feelings.

Starter Pack for Being an Emotionally Mature Leader

SHOW UP

Be the leader you claimed to be. Show up with accomplishments, take responsibility for any lack of accomplishment, take a consistent position on key issues and keep a good conduct. Whenever your attention is needed, show up! Whenever the going gets tough, show up! Whenever encouragement is needed, show up! Whenever the team needs a celebration, show up! SHOW UP all the time.

SPEAK UP

Take the mantle, account for the synergy for innovation and improvement by focusing on what will work alone.

Take risks, look for opportunities and let the goals of the team form the biggest part of your interest.

SHUT UP

One of the traits of a good leader is also knowing when to shut up. Whining and complaining taints a leader's reputation and deviates him from the destination ahead. What's more? The team's morale is punctured. Keep the negative thoughts and opinions to yourself and be positive about what you say to your team. When you have a meeting with your team for example, try to talk last so others have the opportunity to speak first, express their feelings, thoughts and even solutions they might have thought of about subjects covered and moreover feel that they are heard. If they can't speak and are not confident that they will be hear, why have the meeting at all? It will be just a waist of everyone's time, right? As Simon Sinek says: "practice, be the last to speak".

LIGHT UP

Whoever wants a boring leader? Imagine having so much workload and there is no one to spice the mood with some humor or fun activities? The person in the best position for this is always the head. Having a mood-lightener coming from the head brings an atmosphere of comfort to team members. Activities like having a good piece of music playing in the background, creating a goofy contest or even bringing in pizza for lunch can increase productivity and raise motivation levels.

GROW UP

"Age is no guarantee of maturity"

~ Lawana Blackwell ~

This is not necessarily about age, but how much you can put aside your personal feelings to accomplish set goals. How a leader responds to conflicts within an organization requires emotional stability, willingness to listen, self-awareness, patience, courage, perseverance, forgiveness, humility, as well as an open mind. No matter the conflict, your challenge as a leader is none other but to keep a pace of growth.

PRO TIP

Show Up!

    Speak Up!

        Shut Up!

            Light Up!

                & GROW!

How Do You Heighten Your Emotional Maturity?

Simple. Start by focusing on becoming aware of your emotions even as you interact with others. Note that you cannot change that which you are not aware of. Examine how you feel, why you feel it and what made you feel that way. Were there contributing factors that you may not have thought about?

Secondly, you want to consciously become aware of how you respond to your feelings in various situations. How about some situations that you respond to and realize that you didn't think about until after a while? Put all of these in retrospection. Ask yourself the same questions; what were you feeling, why and what was your response? This is definitely not an easy record to keep but with practice, it becomes easier. Each time you do this, you will find that you are less controlled by your emotions and you'd be presented with options of well-thought response to situations each time.

Having a journal of your feelings and responses to happenings will help you greatly. You probably are thinking that, "Hey! Great idea but I've got no time for that". I ask you in return, how much do you really want to master your emotions? Or better, how much do you thirst to be able to lead others?

Tim Vancamp

In your pursuit of leading others, make sure you are able to lead yourself first. Take charge of your own emotions and demonstrate credibility to your followers.

Diving into Leadership: Motivating Others

Tim Vancamp

CHAPTER 4:

TEAM

ORIENTATION

Tim Vancamp

Team Orientation

"I prefer to win titles with the team ahead of individual awards or scoring more goals than anyone else. I'm more worried about being a good person than being the best football player in the world. When all this is over, what are you left with? When I retire, I hope I am remembered for being a decent guy."

~ Lionel Messi ~

As a team leader, how inspiring, motivating and results-oriented are you? Maybe you are a leader now because you love what you are doing or because you are doing what you want to be doing, somewhere along the line, you made this decision to serve people. You took control of things under your jurisdiction, knew yourself better, your dreams and desires; then you paid the price to master self-discipline and personal leadership. Great, cool, but... are you a team builder?

Most team leads are zero percent team builders – they usually don't know how to maintain, orientate and build their teams, maybe because many of them have not been able to build one themselves yet? Or haven't they experienced a great team lead? Did they have a good coach available? Did the leaders in the organization take care of preparing the next generation leaders? A pretty much disorganized person will barely know how to structure an effective team orientation. So, what is the way out?

TEAMWORK!

More than ever businesses are moving faster, need adaptations and changes, fast responses to customers, need flexibility, need to be innovate faster and so on. It is of paramount importance businesses and their leaders' breath, stress out and hell yeah even preach collaboration and team work. Effective collaborative teams will tap into the individual strengths of each team member resulting in a product that is greater than the sum of the individual efforts of each.

Teamwork. Preach it! Foster teamwork!

Install team building activities, diversity workshops, retreats, merit systems, processes facilitating project teams and so on. Pave the way for teamwork!

There is no better lesson learned within a group than one which was contributed by every constituent.

Teamwork is one of the most important characteristics of a successful organization. The absence of teamwork could be the bedrock of multiple problems in a group. In this chapter, we are looking at how a leader can bring together the strengths of individuals in his team and put them together to form an invincible team!

"The way a team plays as a whole determines its success. You may have the greatest bunch of individual stars in the world, but if they don't play together, the club won't be worth a dime."

~ Babe Ruth~

Long gone are those days when organizations assigned individual tasks to employees based on their level and leave them to fulfil whatever task it is each person gets. In today's world, organizations have realized the effectiveness of proper teamwork towards individual as well as organizational goals. Going back to the aforementioned quote, Babe Ruth tries to make a very valid point. The way I see it is that even if you pride yourself in hiring the best employees and assign individual tasks to them, it won't yield as much desired results as it would compare to the results that can be gotten when they are united as a team. This whole concept is based on perception though. You would agree with me that it is more comfortable to work with people whom you connect very well with and have a sense of belonging.

Here's one more reason I love diving. It teaches us that we need to help and be helped. Teamwork in every shade. Your buddies have got your back anytime. They watch out for you when you are not watching. They take responsibility for your adventure into the deep water and vice versa. The joint courage is what keeps every diver motivated and enthusiastic.

Teamwork as part of the organizational culture, whether at a company, a diving club, a non-profit organization, a school/university, a research organization, ... starts at the top with the executive leaders. If not taken to heart, nurtured, execute, and preached there, then it has no point to spread it out down the organization. How do you expect people to follow if all they can see is the opposite of what they're told to do? Walk your walk and talk your talk.

Team Orientation: Improving the Workforce Like a Leaderologist

While the term teamwork may sound easy, it is actually a very demanding task to bind a team together. No jokes. In order to channel each member's individual strength with proper organization and consistency, a leader has to understand the needs and expectations of every constituents and bring them to the team level, so everyone can move forward at a uniform pace.

The likely issue here is that what may seem right to Teammate A may be very offensive to Teammate B. Therefore, it is of great necessity that the leader chosen is a mature, understanding and motivating person who can inspire each team member to work together regardless their varying goals, motivations, diversity or social background. The following tips will illustrate how a team can be built to achieve this:

A playing team is a staying team, together!

"All work and no play...." You know the rest! While the relationship shared by team members is meant to be completely professional and work-oriented, it is natural and humane to seek some 'play time' in the middle of serious work and team targets. Dullness vanishes, and productivity is boosted. If you want to rejuvenate your members to keep contributing to the joint goal, then engage them with some fun activities on a regular basis. You can introduce some interesting games to the team and give away prizes or other fun stuff to the winning individuals or pair. The sense of winning in groups is also a dose of motivation to make workers work together and achieve the formal goals.

A team that connects emotionally, works with oneness.

It is of vital importance that a team is built upon an emotional relationship. It is simple logic. If usually I give 70% of my commitment to work with people I don't connect emotionally with, I will definitely give more than my 100% commitment while working with people I share a healthy professional and emotional connection with. Leaders therefore must be able to focus on knowing every member of their team at personal levels. Once in a while, arrange for a weekly or monthly dinner with the team members. Talk to them like a friend. Keep a connection between each other on emotional levels. In the end, who do you think we work best with and trust the most? Indeed!!! You guessed it. In reality we need to understand that a lot of people spend more time at work when awake then even at home, so a good interpersonal relationship and emotional connection with your team members is not a nice to have, it is a must have of paramount importance. Master this well and you'll go great lengths.

A team can only work in "We's"

While a team naturally consists of various individuals with unique expectations and needs per individual, there is really no individual in a team. They are more or less a 'united team'. The team leader in this case plays a very important role as he has to take commitment in addressing each and every member of the team together as 'one'. A simple way this could work is by referring to 'I' as 'We'. For example, while he is supposed to say "I am happy with you", he should say instead "the entire team is happy with what we have achieved together as one big family/team". These small and simple ways of addressing the team during meetings or challenges are surefire ways of sinking in "togetherness" to the minds of every team member. Therefore, if a team performs well, the treat should go equally to everyone. So also, when there is a performance declination, everyone should be motivated equally.

A successful team consists of clarity, commitment & consistency.

Each and every member in a team must have clearly defined goals and targets. That is, each member should have clear terms of what is expected of them when it comes to contributing to the team's success. More so, there should be an inbuilt commitment to strive for the best performance within their capabilities at all time. In order to keep team members committed and consistent however, the team leader is charged with the task to setup regular meetings where team members will be updated and motivated. Organize intra-team competitions, where and when applicable, that bring in a sense of competitive spirit so that team members may churn in their best efforts. In addition, it is highly important that the leader makes sure to give followers any kind of help they may need to improve their performance. Therefore, if you really want to know what they need, you better start working on that connection straight away. Only by knowing exactly what they need, want, what makes them tick... the leader will be able to have them follow and fully committed to perform at their best of abilities for the benefit of the entire team's performance.

By staying together, each member achieves more.

Regardless how active a team member is in a team, if his individual goals are not met, he will get deeply demoralized and may lose all the motivation to work with the team. A financially distressed team member for example will not be able to concentrate on the team's common goal because deep down in his mind, he is looking for money – his focus is therefore split. The leader's role in this case is to constantly remind the entire team how their individual success is imperative to the success of the group or organization. On the flip side though, one of the best ways to fulfil individual goals is by contributing to the success of the team. Well, for some teammates, money is the necessary motivation they want while some only crave for promotion and appreciations. Therefore, a leader is expected to give his employees and team the due reward they deserve be it monetary or non-monetary just to prove to them that teamwork is an advocate of total growth and success.

From all of this, one thing is prominent - **team members need to be comfortable**. The team must be disciplined yet, allowed some level of freedom. Of course, there has to be an element of fun. Many leaders don't realize that fun is a part of team culture and can come in many forms. One good way to instill fun is to form a team name and an accompanying identity that reflects the team's missions or that of his members.

PRO TIP

Here are some great acronyms for T.E.A.M. (authors unknown) that are easy to remember to help you in your quest for excellence in leadership:

Together	*Tolerant*	*Task*
Everyone	*Encourage*	*Execution*
Achieves	*Acknowledge*	*Acknowledgement*
More	*Mindful*	*Message*

Team members must also know how to run effective meetings through the strict rules of an agenda, roles, responsibilities, ground rules and objective-setting procedures. Consequently, effective methods for planning and communications should be reviewed and established. Team members have to be empowered and trusted enough to do their best at tasks. Once they are, they become more action-oriented and stay committed to achieving the common goal. Ultimately, if the leader can guide them to help set their own goals out of this, then they just committed or bought into their own goals. This kind of process will automatically lead to ownership of the derived goals and tasks and thus a higher sense of responsibility as well in order to achieve their own -, the team's goals and in the end the vision of the leader.

Make sure to manage and lead the team well, but avoid micromanagement. Lead by being present, approachable and available in case they need your input or guidance.

Remember that you are dealing with humans and with emotions and certain expectations. If you find that these emotions can lead to trouble in organization and coordination, respond fine and work on it. Let your followers know that you care about them. Their opinion matters to the organization; let them know this too. Your team needs you. Your team needs your efforts and orientation. Encourage, motivate, reward and recognize.

Create an atmosphere where people enjoy their work. Break the monotony and rotate for example, keep it challenging and interesting, change some work conditions, install a positive work culture. Spend less time in meetings and more on action. Provide tools and equipment to raise the productivity of the team and foresee courses and improvement options. And don't forget to reach out to employees by seeking them out, don't wait for them to come to you. Show that you are accessible to serve wherever you can for the best of the team. In the end you reach the set forward vision only when the team follows you on the path to achievement. It's all in the team, it's all in you leading the team and you need to know every single one of them... personally.

I put it all in a wrap with a quote of Bill Bradley:

"Respect your fellow human being, treat them fairly, disagree with them honestly, enjoy their friendship, explore your thoughts about one another candidly, work together for a common goal and help one another achieve it."

~ Bill Bradley ~

Tim Vancamp

CHAPTER 5:

EMPATHY

Tim Vancamp

Empathy

"When you show deep empathy toward others, their defensive energy goes down, and positive energy replaces it. That's when you can get more creative in solving problems."

~ Stephen Covey ~

E mpathy – the ability to understand someone else's feelings, thoughts, preferences and point of view – is a critical skill necessary for every member of a management/leadership team. From the leader to the led, empathy is a skill everyone in a team must possess. Here's why:

My view on empathy is that it is not limited to 'feelings' alone. It spans into having a real understanding and insight into teammates' mindset. It is about getting to know every member of a team in some depth so as to identify and understand 'what makes them tick'.

What's the point really?

The key is that the better you know someone, the easier it is to manage them more effectively, communicate on another level, create mutual trust and have followers. Imagine going into the deep blue sea (in the name of diving) with a buddy you know little to nothing about? Will you even have peace of mind while diving? Empathy rings a bell!

In organizations, employees respond well to the manager who springs efforts into getting to know them as an individual. This paints to them a manager, a leader, who can see the world, at least from their own point of view.

About empathy; you simply put yourself in other people's shoes. Chances are, you will get to know them better and help them to get out of tough knots better.

Empathy is a quality of emotional intelligence competency. Generally, there are four clusters of competencies in the field of emotional intelligence namely:

- Self-Awareness
- Self-Management
- Social Awareness
- Relationship Management

Empathy falls under social awareness. This skill is one that reflects someone's ability to put a connection through to others and relate to them in such a way that the end product is a healthy relationship. Of course, without the ability to understand what someone else is going through, our relationships remain lurking in the shadows of the superficial terrain. Worse, our relationships will lack the depth and richness that occur when there is an emotional connection between parties. Opportunity goes missing!

Without empathy, a leader rules his domain without considering how other people might feel or react, or may be thinking. As humans, each of us has differing perspectives even to the smallest of things. We all experience joy, pain, hurt, moods, etc. on different levels. Unfortunately, we become so limited when we take things through the route of our perspective only. It becomes easy to make wrong assumptions and jump right into conclusions. This often is the cause of many misunderstandings, poor morale and even organizational crumbling.

PRO TIP

Let your love shine forth to every member of your team. Value them and make it known! When people feel valued, they feel safe. A safe feeling creates trust.

The Power of Empathy

When empathy comes into the picture for understanding why someone is angry or when a child is acting up, for instance, you might learn that something actually inspired the situation. The person may probably have had a home issue, or their mother is ill or the child has no food to eat or just anything. Instead of reacting to these emotions or trying to be defensive, you can push a few questions about their behavior and emotional state to them. While there may still be needing to discipline the person as consequence of their behavior, using empathy first makes him/her valued and will easily accept responsibility for subsequent actions. Offer solutions or even better help where applicable and or feasible. Help them out of situations they struggle with and they will remember your empathic act forever. Reach out a helping hand, if they succeed, you succeed. Gaining satisfaction out of seeing others fail is not a leadership skill. Leaders want people to succeed and they do this with energy, unselfishness, passion and empathy.

The Fine Line Between Empathy and Compassion

To demonstrate empathy, one must also be compassionate. Compassion means 'to care'. It is that burning desire to alleviate other people's suffering. Therefore, to be empathetic, leaders or potential leaders need to care for the people under their voice otherwise, they will bottle-up their feelings. They will not feel safe to open up to their leaders, and you know what that means? Even if there is a problem in the team's structure, it will be left unnoticed or until the leader himself discovers it. Without compassion, we have no business listening to one another. We would not even bother to inquire about their experience. We would not care what is currently being thought of in their mind or what they feel. We put all the pride and wisdom in ourselves and zone out the entire world. So how do you empathize when you have no face for compassion? Compassion is a necessary component of empathy!

Challenges of Empathy

I. **Attention!** To be empathetic requires that we pay attention. We often get busy within our own selves;

in our heads, thinking about our agenda. Therefore, paying attention to what other people are feeling is not on the to-do list. We need to be more self-aware as well as become aware of others. For instance, when next you ask someone how they are doing, pay close attention to their response, is it believable? Are they really okay as said? Then ask yourself if you care to learn more. If yes, ask them further questions to find out what is going on.

2. **It requires time**. In this fast-paced world, people keep moving without a stop. Empathy requires that we stop whatever we are doing and spend quality time caring. Questions like "Hey, what is going on for you, you look like there is something bothering you?" are sometimes the perfect words of introduction to understanding the mind, feelings or happenings of someone. And whenever you decide to talk about a topic do not postpone it. Postponing it would mean you are not genuinely interested from an empathic or compassionate level.

3. **Self-esteem**. Sometimes, self-esteem gets in the way of empathy. When the mind is busy with negative thoughts, the space to care for other people is really not present any longer. Fact, it may happen that when you think you are empathetic,

you are actually busy thinking about you, if they like you, or if you are not capable of helping them.... Etc.

4. **History lurking around as baggage**. The longer you have known someone, the more likely you have a history with them; also, the harder it is to put the past aside and simply be with them. Often times, you have developed a pre-conditioned response to whatever they have to say or do. You need to be aware of this and put an end to it in order to be able to truly open the connection with that person. Leave that baggage at the door of your mind; it's not easy but hey, try to tell a new story about your relationship. That doesn't mean to give up friendly relationships or so, but there are times and places that work needs to be done without too much personal interest mingling with the efficiency. Nonetheless who works better together than people having a good understanding and friendly relationship? Ask yourself how quickly would you be ready to help your family, friends, ...? Well it could well be that you spend more time with your colleagues, so why wait? Find the emotional courage to move forward and turn negativism, blockades, problems and so on into positivism and go for gold. No one is asking to be best friends, but you can have

a professional, healthy relationship leading others towards that vision.

5. **PRO problem-solver**. Somewhere in your subconscious, you believe that if someone shares something with you, there is an automatic need for you to fix them up! NO. That is not empathy. That is something about you, and not them. It is only your need to impress or be right that is getting in the way of true empathy. It diminishes the person and makes them feel devalued. While you may attempt to fix others when they share their problems with you, always keep an open mind and be a part of the conversation. Know more about them; care more, rather than trying to impress. Be prepared to guide them through the problem-solving process so they learn from your experience and grow. While doing so, you will also grow as a leader.

How to Develop the Leadership Skill of Empathy?

#1 Recognize, accept and appreciate differences

Many of us have different ways of:

- Organizing ourselves and work: ranging from people who have a high preference for **structure** to people who prefer to have a high level of **flexibility**.

- Relating to others: ranging from people who are highly **extroverted** to people who are extremely **introverted**.

- Gathering information: ranging from people who like to have a **practical** approach to those who have a thing for being **creative**.

The reality of it all is that we tend to empathize with people who share similar preference with us. It then becomes a challenge when there are real differences. Starting to recognize, accept and appreciate these differences sets you on a right path to successful leadership.

#2 Ask questions

If you want to get to know your buddy more, you simply ask questions - this is pretty obvious. Why not channel some energy into asking them some focused questions? Ask questions like: *"Jane, how do you prefer to organize your work? Structured, flexible? Is there any way I can assist to improve this for you, so as to fit your personal preferences?"*

These questions could provoke some real insights into your team members' preferences particularly on how they like to be led or managed.

#3 Listening

In any context, one of the key leadership skills is the ability to listen. Many of us don't find it easy to listen well, especially when we are speaking to someone who has a different view, thoughts or feelings towards the subject at hand. If we want to be empathetic, we need to step-aside our own thoughts so that listening to the ideas and feelings of team members would be a breeze.

Empathy is a choice, however needed for great leadership. You have to choose to improve, care and go out of your own way to bridge the gap between differing cultures, generations, religions and so forth. Naturally, empathy allows us to be fully human and give others the permission to reciprocate. More importantly, developing empathy with teammates is an amazing way of building relationships within the team.

PRO TIP

Recognize, accept and embrace differences. Ask questions and be a stellar listener to become an empathetic leader.

Tim Vancamp

CHAPTER 6:

CHARISMA

Tim Vancamp

Charisma

"Being a leader gives you charisma. If you look and study the leaders who have succeeded, that's where charisma comes from, from the leading."

~ Seth Godin ~

W hat is it about certain people that makes us feel drawn to them? Charisma! The dictionary explains to us that charisma is a divinely conferred gift or power that gives an individual authority of influence over a large number of people. Of course, we see that a lot in the movies, politics, culture and business fields, but where does charisma come from, and are we born with it?

When jobs of high caliber such as CEO, COO and President need a new person in power, there are many qualities to be considered in an applicant. Conventionally, the team considers an applicant's qualities such as capability, education and experience. But the quality that is most likely to facilitate high-end positions is that part of some personalities called charisma.

Not everyone is gifted with charisma. A charismatic person is not someone who turns up and everyone start shivering frightenedly. That is a dictator, not a charismatic leader. Interestingly there is no antonym for charisma. Probably, because charisma itself is already hard to define.

The most successful people in starring roles in society have charisma or tact, or both. People with the former immediately secure other people's loyalty almost at first-sight, with or without so many desirable assets. People with tact are able to instinctively grasp the situation at hand and put everyone at ease by being able to say the right thing just when it is most appropriate. Also, they lead others to act positively and ease difficult situations. The relationship between tact and charisma is a worthy one. See tact as other leadership skills we have, since been discussing earlier in this book while charisma as the crowd-pulling recipe.

A charismatic person connects with people right away on almost every level of life – physically, intellectually and yes, emotionally. Charisma has been a characteristic of many leaders who had crowds following them because people feel strongly attached to a charismatic person. So you could somehow say that charisma results from inspiring leadership.

You too can have charisma

Now, close your eyes and think deep. Do you know anyone that everyone seems to be drawn to? You have been watching this person as he moves around attracting, chatting and making friends with as many people as he could. That's charisma staring at you in the face dear reader.

The magic: when charismatic people enter a room, their mere presence sparks up some attention-pulling audience. Their energy may even lighten up the entire gathering. The very core of charisma is *a basic self-confidence and the ability to pass it on to others*.

Charisma is guaranteed when one person promotes positive energy with other people. People will look up to you for your good vibes; they will respect you, they will say they find you charismatic once you begin to give off waves of charisma. Anyone can be a promoter of good vibes. Not everyone is charismatic, but anyone can be. Somehow one could say that charisma is a gene of our leadership DNA, but it's just in a latent state, waiting to be developed into a fully functional unit.

To develop charisma, you only need to learn the models of a charismatic person and how they think. For then will you be able to inspire people, persuade them to see things as they should and ignite their enthusiasm. Or what is a leader without loyal followers?

10 Powerful Ways to Attract Charisma

1. **Self-awareness:** Start paying more attention to how you feel, your actions and reactions to different situations in your life. Have a mental note of your feelings and your body language in situations. Self-awareness is an essential assessment tool needed just before we can control others perception of us.

2. **Elevate your mood**: It is hardly possible not to have an elevation of mood when we encounter someone that is happy. Speak and act in a cheerful mood and you would see how people will love to associate with you. If you want to improve your mood, start by exercising. Exercise is an excellent way to optimize your health, improve how you feel as well as longevity. Exercise also stimulates the release of mood-enhancers (endorphins) into the body. Also practicing your favorite hobby(ies) regularly can help elevate your mood and energy. In essence, do what livens up your own mood 99% of the time.

PRO TIP:

A cheerful mood is a contagious and a very powerful way to make yourself more magnetic.

---

3. **What's in it for them:** Do your best to make people feel important. While you cannot please everyone, try as much to make them feel as though they are the most important person in the room. If you yearn to be charismatic, invest your time in listening and getting to know people. Make sure they can see the added value and most importantly from their side is: *"what is in it for me?"* Make it a win-win situation. And NO it is not just about the money. As mentioned earlier, figure out what makes them tick. A good question to start from: "Why should they be proud, energized, happy to be working in my team, in our organization?"

4. **Speak knowledge:** It is okay to flaunt your knowledge. As some will put it: *knowledge is sexy.* We all have that special knowledge of something; it could be an interest or a skill. Let other people know what excites you and what motivates you to get up every day. Of course, you would have to share

your ideas and convictions in conversations. Don't force it! Show people that you are a leader with a sense of direction.

PRO TIP

Be careful when communicating. Keep facts and opinions separate in order to maintain your credibility.

---

5. **Improve your look:** Have an alluring appearance. Keep your personal hygiene in top shape and dress to express how great you feel about yourself. Don't push it too. Dress the best that your financial resources can handle. Keep things simple and have your clothes tailored to give a sharp look. In short: "Dress for success."

6. **Show sincere empathy:** Conveying empathy is a personal-magnetism booster. If you want to pull a crowd, sincere empathy is probably the most important attribute you can display. If people feel that you don't understand them or how they feel, it may be very difficult influencing them.

7. **Be a storyteller:** Your story has value, tell it! Everyone loves a good story. Stories have a way of making events and occurrences memorable, aids learning and makes the storyteller an interesting person. Some people have honed their storytelling skills in such that they have a new story to tell each time. You can even throw in some anecdotes, similes, analogies, metaphors and even contrasts.

8. **Make their name a priority:** It feels good to hear your name in conversations, from speakers and just any good source. When you are conversing, say your audience's name in the introduction as well as when you are finished talking to them. Do a personal rand recall for them; they will love to hear you speak more.

9. **Show gratitude:** Appreciate what you have as this is key to being in a cheerful disposition at all times. As aforementioned, this is necessary to attract people.

10. **Be funny:** Blunt and true. People love wit, humor and maybe a little bit of sarcasm? Learn your personal style of using humor and apply it when appropriate to keep your audience interested. Do not overdue it in order not to look ridiculous.

11. **Communicate effectively:** Use an animated voice by varying the volume of your voice and utilizing intended breaks or pauses to emphasize important points. Express emotions like for example surprise, happiness, sadness and the more, along with the message itself so people can hear you are emotionally connected. Furthermore, your facial expressions may alter the message at least when it is at par with your emotions and the message you want to convey like for example: frowning, smiling, looking surprised etc. Eye contact speaks for itself, and all of this can be reinforced by deliberate use of gestures. But be careful with gestures as they might seem clumsy, unnatural, too much or too theatrical when not controlled well.

Charisma! Charisma! It doesn't make you a crafty trickster that pulls wool of over people's eyes. Instead, it unleashes a part of you that people will find accommodating and will naturally want to be on your side all through your tenure to lead them.

Do understand that charisma is a powerful trait in motivating, but ensure your team that it is not just you who is the success of the team, or company. Charisma is not about your success as a leader. You need to have the best intentions of the organization at heart and have the other qualities, already mentioned in this book, in order to justify yourself as a leader. Don't fall into the trap to only be charismatic. People will figure it out quickly and may not follow. Show your other leadership skills and traits as well, charisma alone is not enough!

Tim Vancamp

FINAL NOTES

Tim Vancamp

Final Notes

Leadership is not about holding a certain position and it certainly **does not come with a job title.**

Leadership is surrounded with a lot of confusion, as there is no clear archetype available of a leader and the term itself is used in very different contexts. Just take a look around and ask different people to clarify what they think leadership is and you'll be surprised, or not, how many different definitions and clarifications you'll receive. But as clarified in this book there are some common traits and skills leaders possess. Leadership or being a leader is all about *who you are*, *how you do* things and *what you do*, as you probably have figured out by now. Thus, it is your mindset and your attitude that will define you as a leader.

Be authentic, again there are is no archetype available, and if you have a vision and are able to convey that vision and inspire people toward working to that vision, then you have chosen to be a leader today. And don't get me wrong, I didn't say it is a one time off of training or coaching session you'll have to attend to be a leader. No, no, no, it is a lifelong journey of learning, reflecting, adapting and improving yourself to become the better unique you.

Leadership is kind of a big deal. Are you ready to do what it takes? Of course, there is a lot to learn but there are fun ways to do it. One of the most enjoyable ways to experience and learn about leadership naturally and almost unconsciously is by scuba diving. No jokes!

A lot of what were covered in this book will be taught and most of the time, self-taught all through one's diving experience. It takes courage and mindset to be a leader; a true one.

Remember that every leader is called to serve. You are not also ordering a team but joining it. You are not a boss, but a team lead. A leader empathizes with his team members while he also works actively to the best interest of the team's mission.

Boss, No. Leader, YES!

Start your leadership journey today, act towards the better YOU. As time passes by, day by day, you will be you in a year, two years and soon from now, but you will be more confident, you will have evolved your leadership skills and style. As explained it is an ongoing journey and it requires daily practice. Here are some practical tips to get you started and do use the blank pages at the end of the book to write down more as you go along or even your progress or priority list. It can make a nice list to reflect on whenever you want to in the future.

Some practical tips to start today:

- Stop micromanaging.
- Say good morning every day with a genuine smile.
- Mentor someone.
- Get a mentor.
- Motivate someone.
- Think of a mantra and write it down in this book.
- Volunteer to do something counterintuitive.
- Ask for help.
- Ask if you can help someone, even if it is out of your comfort zone.
- Try to use some other means of transportation to your work or use another route.

- Put someone in the spotlight, congratulate him/her in the open during a meeting for example.

- Start structuring your meetings and make them more effective.

- Start reducing the number of meetings.

- Introduce a problem-solving process or find someone to help you with that.

- Meet someone you don't know yet, out of your inner-circle or connections.

- Start reading a business magazine, a biography, a magazine of a totally different perspective than what you are used to.

- Keep the technology you use updated with the current releases and when out of date, replace the hardware.

- Work on your discipline.

- Get some advice on your clothing style for different occasions.

- Follow your intuition.

- Smile more today and greet people with a smile.

- Listen more than you talk today.

- Ask more questions today.

- Subscribe for a course, class outside your expertise.

- Fight for your team, your people.

- Avoid any negativism today.
- Plan, set the goals and try to meticulously execute it.
- Strive to be consistent.
- Be honest.
- Set up a team event outside the organization to create comradery and togetherness.
- Have lunch with one of your team members, your supervisor, someone from another division, ...
- Organize a diner with your team.
- Make sure to be on time for meetings, appointments, your family party, for diner at home.
- Work on your empathy.
- Ask feedback on where you are as a leader today and revisit it in a year or so.
- Plan your leadership skills improvements at the end of this book.
- Add more things to this list as of today:
- ....
- ....
- ....
- ....
- ....
- ....

Tim Vancamp

PRO TIPS

IN A ROW

Tim Vancamp

11 **PRO TIPS in a row...**

- *Divers plan their dive and dive their plan! Effective planning and meticulous execution actively creates energy.*

- *Leaders communicate and keep communicating. Just when they think they have communicated enough, they feel as though they need to communicate more. Effective communication actively creates energy.*

- *Be consistent by conscious choice in your words, behaviors and actions. Be honest in those three as well and strive for your "wholeness" (integer in Latin means whole and complete). People will notice you are in integrity.*

- *Probe yourself with any question you wish to have an answer to. For example, "What exactly is my life goal?", "How can I achieve this goal?", "What should I do right now to resolve this issue?"*

- *Always remember that when attempting to motivate other people, your feelings mean less to them than their feelings.*

- *Show Up! Speak Up! Shut Up! Light Up! & GROW!*

- *Here are some great acronyms for T.E.A.M. (authors unknown) that are easy to remember to help you in your quest for excellence in leadership:*

  o **T**ogether **E**veryone **A**chieves **M**ore

  o **T**olerant **E**ncourage **A**cknowledge **M**indful

  o **T**ask **E**xecution **A**cknowledgement **M**essage

- *Let your love shine forth to every member of your team. Value them and make it known! When people feel valued, they feel safe. A safe feeling enables trust.*

- *Recognize, accept and embrace differences. Ask questions and be a stellar listener to become an empathetic leader.*

- *A cheerful mood is a contagious and a very powerful way to make yourself more magnetic.*

- *Be careful when communicating. Keep facts and opinions separate in order to maintain your credibility.*

Finally, I leave you with this quote from the COO of Facebook:

"Leadership is about making others better as a result of your presence and making sure that impact lasts in your absence"

~ Sheryl Sandberg~

YOU will LEAD better!

YOU LEAD!

Tim Vancamp

Appendix

Tim Vancamp

Quotes in a row:

Now that you've read *Diving Into Leadership: Motivating Others*, you can find the quotes below that were mentioned in this book so you can easily find them in case you want to refresh your memory.

1) Tim Vancamp:
   As I headed out for a night dive, I saw the sunset-colored waves extinguish on the beach, but with subdued memories I can see your sun rays surfing the sea towards me. Far away but always near me.

2) Unknown:
   I dive because I'd rather look back at life, saying "I can't believe I did that" instead of "if only I had."

3) Paul Coelho:
   When you are enthusiastic about what you do, you feel this positive energy. It's that simple.

4) Paul Polman:
   Leadership is not just about giving energy... it's unleashing other people's energy.

5) **John C. Maxwell:**
   The best leaders are readers of people. They have the intuitive ability to understand others by discerning how they feel and recognizing what they sense.

6) **Steve Jobs:**
   It doesn't make sense to hire smart people and then tell them what to do: we hire smart people, so they can tell us what to do.

7) **Ronnie Lampole:**
   If you need a moment to think. Go diving and you will have a few minutes of peace and quiet.

8) **Samuel Ullman:**
   Maturity is the ability to think, speak and act your feelings within the bounds of dignity. The measure of your maturity is how spiritual you become during the midst of your frustrations.

9) **Lawana Blackwell:**
   Age is no guarantee for maturity.

10) Lionel Messi:

I prefer to win titles with the team ahead of individual awards or scoring more goals than anyone else. I´m more worried about being a good person than being the best football player in the world. When all this is over, what are you left with? When I retire, I hope I am remembered for being a decent guy.

11) Babe Ruth:

The way a team plays as a whole determines its success. You may have the greatest bunch of individual stars in the world, but if they don't play together, the club won't be worth a dime.

12) Bill Bradley:

Respect your fellow human being, treat them fairly, disagree with them honestly, enjoy their friendship, explore your thoughts about one another candidly, work together for a common goal and help one another achieve it.

13) Stephen Covey:

When you show deep empathy towards others, their defensive energy goes down, and positive energy replaces it. That's when you can get more creative in solving problems.

14) Seth Godin:

Being a leader gives you charisma. If you look and study the leaders who have succeeded, that's where charisma comes from, from the leading.

15) Sheryl Sandberg:

Leadership is about making others better as a result of your presence and making sure that impact lasts in your absence.

Diving into Leadership: Motivating Others

Tim Vancamp

Photo Credits

Credit and appreciation go out to the below mentioned photographers. You can also find the title they gave to their photos and the description, if any, is placed in italic.

Dedication: photo by Tim Vancamp. Title: Moonrise at Isla de mar, in Tossa de Mar.

Chapter 1: photo by Samara Doole. Title: Splah 2. *Because the ocean is the best.*

Chapter 2: photo by Linus Nylund. Title: Good morning. *Waking up at 5.30 we entered the water just as the sun was rising. Even in a busy place there is always a time when most people are sleeping and you can find a tranquil moment for yourself.*

Chapter 3: adapted from photo by Paul Gilmore. Title: Self portrait.

Chapter 4: photo by Sharon Pittaway. Title: Water lightbulb.

Chapter 5: photo by Amy Humphries. Title: Bubble hands.

Chapter 6: adapted from photo by Jeremy Bishop. Title: Deep Blue.

Final Notes: photo by Jiyad Nassar. Title: love.

Pro Tips in a Row: adapted from a photo by Hunters Race. Title: The Boss. *This is a shot of the owner of New Zealand watch company - Hunters Race.*

Appendix: photo by Ryan Searle. Title: Sunset at Clevedon Pier.

Tim Vancamp

Index

G

H

N

O

P

U

V

W

Y

Z

Tim Vancamp

About the Author

Tim Vancamp was born and raised in Mol, Belgium. He started his career as the owner of a fitness center together with one of his brothers. Then he started to combine this with a sales representative profession for a medical distributor in Belgium after three years. Two years further down the road he fully threw himself into the medical device industry when he moved up at the distributor to lead and manage the whole pain portfolio for that company. Together with the owner and CEO they grew the portfolio out to be the most successful one held at the company in a range of medical device specialties at that time.

Tim took the step to join St. Jude Medical, Inc. mid 2006. There he moved up the ranks, holding and some even starting up new, positions in sales, marketing and education. After St. Jude Medical he held a position as Vice President Business Development at a startup company in the neuromodulation industry and is now actively involved in the vagal nerve stimulation industry. He always had a broad perspective on the business wanting to know as many aspects as possible and aid where he could. His innovative mindset has led to several industry-first initiatives in an effort to support and educate healthcare professionals for the benefit of patients as well as to grow the business.

With his passion, perseverance and acumen he has played a key role in developing a novel stimulation design which was incepted by Professor Dr. Dirk De Ridder, who currently holds the Neurological Foundation Chair in Neurosurgery at the Department of Surgical Sciences at the Dunedin School of Medicine in Otago, New Zealand. This has been probably one of the most groundbreaking developments in the history of neuromodulation and even today is a more and more selected treatment option to aid patients all over the world. For over 10 years they researched the novel stimulation design called burst stimulation with world premieres like treating tinnitus with cortical (burst) stimulation and even, serendipitously, through the means of stimulation, finding the place in the brain that induces an out-of-body experience. They took their research even beyond just this novel stimulation design and new treatments for several new to the neuromodulation world indications, by already exploring other types of stimulation designs and indications.

Tim has (co-)authored and published numerous peer-reviewed articles in medical journals on neuromodulation topics and co-written several book chapters, has presented even more posters at national and international congresses and has been an invited speaker at some of those as well.

He has nearly two decades experience in the medical device industry growing into higher positions with expanded responsibilities and territories within start-up and multinational environments.

As a med tech executive, author, public speaker and avid diver, he is a master scuba diver and holds several specializations in diving as well, Tim's mantra is: "Be ready to dive into the unexpected and be open to grab opportunities, learn, implement, help and coach, and be ready to challenge the current state of things to improve what you can influence or to help others, as leaders do. Be passionate about what you do, shine the spotlight on your team and celebrate victories. No passion, no fun, ..., no glory."

Tim currently lives with his family near Barcelona in Spain.

Tim Vancamp

Diving into Leadership: Motivating Others

Tim Vancamp

Diving into Leadership: Motivating Others

Tim Vancamp